W9-CFF-862

WITHDRAWN

BCH
JNF

CHEROKEE
JUN 6 - 1990

EARTHQUAKES
Looking for Answers

Margaret Poynter

CHEROKEE

JUN 6 - 1990

—an Earth Processes book—

E N S L O W P U B L I S H E R S, I N C.

Bloy St. & Ramsey Ave.   P.O. Box 38

Box 777   Aldershot

Hillside, N.J. 07205   Hants GU12 6BP

U.S.A.   U.K.

Copyright © 1990 by Margaret Poynter.

All rights reserved.

No part of this book may be reproduced by any means
without the written permission of the publisher.

Library of Congress Cataloging-in-Publication Data

Poynter, Margaret
    Earthquakes: looking for answers / Margaret Poynter.
        p. cm. —(An Earth processes book)
    Summary: Describes what is known about earthquake predicting and also discusses causes and measurements of earthquakes and tsunamis.
    ISBN 0-89490-274-1
    1. Earthquakes—Juvenile literature. 2. Earthquake prediction—Juvenile literature. 3. Tsunamis—Juvenile literature.
[1. Earthquake prediction. 2. Earthquakes.] I. Title.
II. Series.
QE521.3.P68 1990
551.2'2—dc20
                                                                        89—36403
                                                                              CIP
                                                                               AC
Printed in the United States of America

10 9 8 7 6 5 4 3 2 1

Illustrations Courtesy of:
California Institute of Technology, pp. 18, 20, 54, 58; Department of Library Services, American Museum of Natural History, pp. 9, 29, 31, 52; Jet Propulsion Laboratory, p. 46; Gary McCarthy, pp. 49, 50; National Oceanic and Atmospheric Administration, pp. 33, 35, 38; U.S. Geological Survey, pp. 19, 32.

Cover Photograph:
Courtesy of California Institute of Technology

Contents

1

Looking for Answers

On the evening of December 10, 1811, the residents of New Madrid, Missouri, went to bed. A few hours later, at almost 2 A.M., there was a sharp jolt. People were thrown onto the floor and furniture was overturned. A few victims were crushed beneath the falling debris. Most managed to find their way to the outdoors. Stumbling and running, they ran to the nearby fields. The ground rolled and swelled beneath their feet. Trees whipped to and fro as if caught in the winds of a hurricane.

The survivors huddled together, praying they would be alive when the sun rose. The ground continued to convulse and shudder. Thirty minutes after the first jolt, there came another. Like a mighty wave, the earth heaved. Log cabins splintered and fell. The chill air was filled with the screams of terrified people.

Daybreak finally came, but the sun was hidden by a foul-smelling black haze. There were great holes and ditches where there had once been fields and meadows. The Mississippi River, which bordered the town, was swollen. Its water was thick and red. Mud had been tossed from the riverbed to the surface.

At 7 A.M. another major jolt struck the stunned survivors. More deep chasms appeared in the ground. From these chasms came hissing

5

geysers of steam. Then mixtures of mud, sand, and coal dust rose to heights of 100 to 200 feet (30 to 60 m). Entire forests were destroyed. The trees fell in orderly rows, like carefully placed dominoes. Flashes of lightning appeared in the sky.

Meanwhile, up and down the river, hills and bluffs were breaking apart and sliding into the river. Entire islands sank into the water. Some boats were thrown onto high ground. Other boats were swamped by walls of water that suddenly appeared before them.

The crew members of the paddle wheeler *New Orleans* tried to make their way down the river to safety. Suddenly a wall of mud appeared before them. It stretched from one side of the river to the other. From this wall, a monstrous wave thundered up the river toward them. Miraculously the *New Orleans* survived the ordeal. Its crew lived to tell of the day that the Mississippi River had flowed backward.

The New Madrid earthquake caused damage over an area of 50,000 square miles (80,000 square km). It changed the course of several rivers and streams. It created new lakes while swallowing up old ones. It felled forests and covered fertile fields with sand.

Its tremors were felt as far south as the Gulf Coast and as far north as Canada, over an area of 1,000,000 square miles (2,600,000 square km).

Some Early Answers

Why does the earth move? From the time people first felt the ground tremble, they tried to answer that question. Many primitive peoples thought that the earth rested upon the back of some sort of animal. When that animal became restless, great cracks appeared in the ground, and tall trees swayed and fell. In South America, the animal was a whale. In Japan, it was a great black spider or a giant catfish. One ancient tribe thought that four bulls supported the earth on their horns. To amuse themselves, they sometimes tossed it from one to another.

The Chinese believed that the monsters lived in caves *inside* the earth. When the creatures fought, the surface of the earth trembled.

In Greece, it was not an animal, but a Titan named Atlas who was condemned to support the world upon his shoulders. Later, about the third century B.C., a Greek philosopher, Aristotle, had a more scientific explanation for earthquakes. He thought that they occurred when hot air masses tried to escape from the center of the earth. Two centuries later, Lucretius, a Roman, wrote that underground landslides caused the earth's surface to move.

The Search for Answers Continues

Many centuries passed. Many more myths arose. But the mystery surrounding earthquakes remained unsolved. Then, in the middle 1800s, Robert Mallet, an engineer, began his study of major earthquakes. He drew a world map that showed the areas where most of the *seismic*, or earthquake, activity occurred. He was the first to use the word *seismology*, which means the science of earthquakes.

Mallet used blasting powder to create his own earth tremors. He measured the distance the seismic waves traveled. He also noted the time it took them to reach a certain point. His measurements told him that the waves traveled at one speed when they were going through sandy material. And they traveled at another speed when they were passing through dense or closely packed material, such as solid rock.

At that time, many people thought that underground explosions were the cause of earthquakes. But Mallet knew that rock can break under stress. He was the first to believe that earthquakes result when rock has become overstressed.

Very few scientists believed that Mallet was right. It was said that no one would ever discover the cause of earthquakes. Why? Because these violent convulsions occur out of sight, far below the earth's surface.

One man said that maybe someone *would* find the cause of earthquakes. But it wouldn't be Mallet. His reason? Mallet was Irish, and a major earthquake had never been recorded in Ireland.

John Milne, an English geologist, was one of the few who agreed with Mallet. Milne also set off his own earth tremors. Sometimes he used explosives. Sometimes he dropped a heavy iron ball from a great height. He measured the tremors with a homemade *seismograph*. This earthquake-measuring device consisted of a *stylus*, or needle, that hung from a pendulum. When the ground shook, the stylus made up-and-down scratches on a glass plate.

As time passed, better seismographs were invented. The markings they made were called *seismograms*. Seismographic stations were set up in many parts of the world. Scientists studied the areas where there were many earthquakes. They found that many of these areas contained major faults. *Faults* are great cracks in the earth's crust. Each side of the fault is lined with huge blocks of rock.

Now there was an important question to be answered. Do faults cause earthquakes, or do earthquakes cause faults?

Powerful, Unseen Forces

The San Andreas Fault runs almost the entire length of California. The city of San Francisco is located near that fault. During the late 1800s it was shaken by hundreds of small earthquakes. Then in 1906, it was devastated by a violent earthquake and the fires that followed. Thirty thousand buildings were destroyed. Half of the city's population was left without homes. The death toll was 667.

In 1911, Harry Reid, an engineer, studied the site of the San Francisco earthquake. He saw a road that had been torn in half. The west side of the road had moved several feet to the north. The east side has moved in a southerly direction. This road lay along the fault line.

Reid also found that some sections of the ground along the fault had moved *before* the earthquake. The movement had taken place slowly, over long periods of time. Reid realized that there are powerful forces at work along the fault line. These forces are constantly tugging, pushing, and pulling the two sides of the fault in opposite directions.

Reid decided that the fault was the cause, not the result of the earthquake. But after all those years of pushing and pulling, why does the earthquake finally occur? Reid answered that question. Facing blocks of rock are shoved together. The underground forces try to move them in opposite directions. But friction acts as a glue, making the blocks stick together. They are put under increasing strain. The rock is twisted out of shape.

Eventually, the strain overcomes the friction. Like a rubber band that is stretched and then released, the rock twangs back into shape. At that time, there is a series of jarring, jolting seismic waves.

Reid was convinced that he had discovered the cause of earthquakes. But many scientists did not agree with his ideas. They said there were too many unanswered questions. Why does the earth move along fault lines? What sort of forces are at work beneath the

The 1906 earthquake and succeeding fires devastated the city of San Francisco.

earth's surface? Why are there fault lines in some places and not in others? And what causes aftershocks, the tremors that follow the first earthquake?

Reid continued to look for answers to these questions. Meanwhile, other scientists were getting information from people who had survived a strong earthquake. They found out what these people had felt as the ground rolled beneath their feet.

"First, there was a sudden jolt that made me lose my balance for a second," one of them said. "Then I could feel the ground moving, and a second, stronger jolt came. After a few seconds of shaking, a rolling and swaying motion started, like being on a boat. The swaying lasted until the earthquake ended. There was noise all the time."

Scientists also studied the seismograms of different earthquakes. The zigzag lines showed them that there are different kinds of seismic waves. The P, or primary waves, travel at great speeds, so they appear first. P waves compress and expand the material in their path, with a push-pull action. P waves can travel through any type of material, liquid or solid. They move buildings back and forth in a rolling motion and can cause chasms to open in the earth.

The S, or secondary waves, jerk and jiggle particles of rock up and down and from side to side. Their action shakes buildings up and down and sideways. S waves travel more slowly than P waves, but often cause more damage to structures. They cannot travel through liquids.

At the onset of a strong earthquake, there is often a roar like the sound of an express train. It's caused by P or S waves that have reached the earth's surface and are traveling through the air. The motion of these surface waves is like that of an ocean wave or a rippling flag. They travel slowly, but may circle the earth many times before dying out. Their action can cause disturbances in oceans and lakes that are located far from the area in which the earthquake occurred.

P waves cause a smooth up-and-down line on a seismogram. S waves cause the needle to swing wildly, making a ragged pattern. The length of time between the arrival of the P and S waves gives an indication of where the focus of the earthquake is. If the S waves closely follow the P waves, the focus is not far from the location of the seismograph. If the S waves arrive much later than the P waves, the focus is far away.

The Study of Inner Space

Andrija Mohorovicic was born in what is now Yugoslavia. In 1909, he was studying the seismograms of a minor European earthquake. He saw that when the seismic waves were close to the earth's surface, they traveled at one speed. But when they were further underground, they traveled faster.

Mohorovicic knew that seismic waves travel faster or slower according to the material through which they are passing. He concluded that there is a layer of dense material several miles beneath the earth's surface.

Mohorovicic's discovery had let him take a peek into a region that had always been hidden from view. Other scientists used seismic waves to take their own looks into inner space. They found that the earth can be compared to a hard-boiled egg. An egg is surrounded by a thin, fragile shell. The earth is surrounded by a thin layer of material known as the crust. The continental crust, which forms our continents, is 20 to 35 miles thick (32 to 56 km). The oceanic crust, which forms our ocean floor, is 3 to 5 miles thick (5 to 8 km).

The earth's crust is not one continuous piece of material. It's divided into at least seven large plates, or slabs, and several smaller ones. The bottoms of the plates are rooted in the mantle, which can be compared to the white part of the hardboiled egg. The mantle is 1,800 miles thick (2,900 km). It is made of rock that is rich in iron and magnesium.

The temperature inside the earth is very high. The heat causes the mantle to be soft, like very thick tar. It is soft enough to move. As the mantle moves, so do the plates.

In the center of an egg, there is a yolk. In the center of the earth, there is a core with a radius of 2,200 miles (3,500 km). The core has two layers. The inner layer is hard. The outer layer is liquid. It moves much more easily than the material in the mantle.

The heat inside the movable layers of the earth travels by means of convection currents. Convection currents can be seen in a clear glass pot of boiling water. They start at the bottom of the pot, where the source of the heat is located. Then they rise to the top, separate, and go in opposite directions.

Parts of the bottom of the mantle are hot enough to set up convection currents. The currents travel to the top of the mantle. Here, they separate. As they move away from each other along this divergent boundary, they pull sections of plate apart. Molten material bubbles up and erupts into the gap that is left. When this material hardens, it forms new oceanic crust.

New ocean crust is formed along these divergent boundaries.

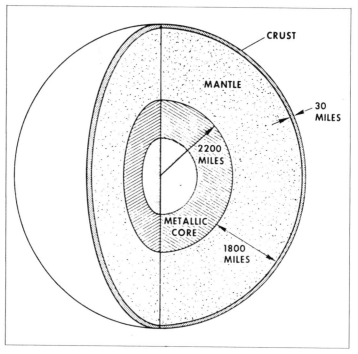

A cross section of the earth showing the core, mantle, and crust.

Sections of old plate are moving apart at that point. So what happens to the older outer margins of crust on the other side of the plate? If nothing happens to the old crust, the seafloor and thus the world would keep getting bigger. But the world *isn't* getting bigger. Somewhere, the old crust is disappearing.

Where is this disappearance taking place? It takes place along convergent boundaries in the deep undersea trenches that border the Pacific, Atlantic, and Indian oceans. Within these trenches, the oceanic crust slides under the continental crust. The heat caused by the friction of movement and the heat within the mantle itself melts the oceanic crust. Cooled, downward-moving convection currents carry the soft material deep into the mantle.

Other convergent boundaries are located where two continental plates meet. Here, as they collide head on, great sections of crust may crumple as the hood of a car does when it hits a brick wall. The

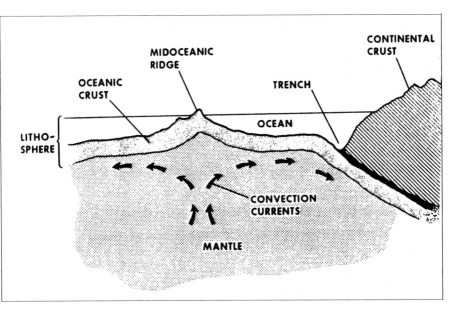

Molten rock from the mantle, heated by the core, rises to the surface, where it cools. Then, it descends, diving beneath the continental crust.

crumpled crust has formed some of our great mountain ranges, including the Himalayas.

A third kind of plate boundary is called a transform boundary. Here, two sections of crust are moving past each other in opposite directions. California's San Andreas Fault is an example of a transform boundary. The western side of that fault is creeping northward, the eastern side southward. The movement is obvious to some of the people who live in the middle of the fault. They can see how their curbstones and house foundations are crumbling and swerving.

In contrast, the movement of the earth's large plates is so slow that it's hard to notice during a human lifetime. But over millions of years it has caused the face of our planet to change drastically. Take a close look at a world map. The bulge on the western side of Africa could fit neatly into the eastern side of Central America. The eastern tip of Antarctica could nestle into the western tip of Australia. Such clues led researchers to realize that these bodies of land were once joined together.

The forces inside our earth are always at work. They cause sections of crust to pull away from each other. They cause other sections to move past each other in opposite directions. Entire plates may move toward each other and collide.

During all of this movement, huge sections of rock are scraping against each other. There is a great deal of friction. The rock becomes stressed. Eventually, it becomes overstressed. That is when an earthquake occurs.

2

The Science of Earthquakes

Robert Mallet, John Milne, and Harry Reid were pioneers in the study of earthquakes. Today, seismologists all over the world are still gathering information about the forces that cause earthquakes. They have learned that each earthquake is different from every other earthquake. Each one has its own set of triggers that set it off. Some are very destructive, and many are so slight they barely register on a seismograph.

Seismologists know that most earthquakes occur in certain parts of the world. They also know that the earth can shake in areas where such movement is least expected.

The earth's movements are often confusing. To unravel their mysteries, seismologists study the earthquakes that occur every day. They try to predict the earthquakes that may occur in the future. And they examine the earth's features to discover what caused the earthquakes of the distant past. The secrets they uncover tell them much about our planet's history, its present, and its future.

The Language of Seismology

There are certain words that are used again and again when earthquakes are being discussed. One of these words is temblor, which means earthquake. Temblor is often used in newspapers and on television and radio. It is not, however, used by seismologists. The following words *are* used by seismologists.

The *focus* of an earthquake is the place where the earthquake begins. It is here that the rock actually slips along a fault. The focus may be confined to a very small area, or it may extend for several miles or kilometers. The focus is usually well below the earth's surface. Sometimes, though, it is located on the surface. The closer to the surface the focus is, the stronger the earthquake will seem to the people in the area.

The strongest shaking will often occur directly above the focus. This surface location is called the *epicenter*. However, the place where the fault breaks the surface may be, sometimes, the greatest area of shaking and damage.

The *intensity* of an earthquake is measured by the amount of damage it causes. Intensity is also measured by what people see and feel during the quake. Thus, an earthquake on the ocean floor always has a very low intensity.

When the epicenter is near a populated area, it will probably be of high intensity. Strong quakes may topple buildings. People may be injured. They may need food, clothes, shelter, and medical attention.

The intensity may be very high if structures are built upon layers of loose, damp soil. When this type of soil is shaken by a violent earthquake, it may turn into an oozy substance like a very thick liquid. This process is called *liquefaction*. Liquefaction can cause buildings to sink or to topple over. It can cause landslides. Much of the destruction caused by the 1906 San Francisco earthquake was due to liquefaction. In the 1964 Alaska earthquake, liquefaction caused huge bluffs to slide into the sea, carrying houses and people with them.

The actual strength or size of an earthquake wave is measured in terms of *magnitude*. Around the world, hundreds of seismographs record earth tremors. Seismologists study these records. By using computers, they can locate the focus. They also determine its magnitude. If the magnitude is high and the epicenter is near a populated area, the seismologists will alert rescue agencies.

After a strong earthquake, there are usually several more quakes. These *aftershocks* occur as the rock adjusts to its new position. They can be nearly as strong as the original jolt. Following one earthquake in Japan, seismographs recorded 1,256 aftershocks. More than 200 of them were strong enough to frighten the people in the region.

Measuring Earthquakes

By the late 1860s, seismology was being studied by people in many countries. But there was still no agreement about how to measure the strength of an earthquake. Each country used a different scale to measure intensity. In Australia, one degree of intensity was equal to the shaking of a house when a horse rubbed against the veranda.

In 1902, Guiseppe Mercalli, an Italian geologist, developed an intensity scale that came into worldwide use. In 1931, it was expanded to include such things as automobiles and very tall buildings.

To people near the epicenter of an earthquake, the shaking may feel very strong. To people many miles from the epicenter, the shaking will seem weak, and at each location there will be different amounts of damage. Thus, one earthquake may have several degrees of intensity.

In contrast, each earthquake has only one magnitude. In 1937, Dr. Charles Richter developed the Richter scale, which indicates magnitude. The scale starts at 0. It has no top figure, because no one knows how strong an earthquake can be. Most earthquakes that are strong enough to be recorded register between 3 and 8 on the Richter scale. The two strongest recorded earthquakes were the 1960 earthquake in Chile and the 1964 earthquake in Alaska. Both registered well over 8 on the Richter scale.

Each number on the Richter scale represents ten times more energy than the number just below it. Thus, a magnitude of 8 is ten times greater than a magnitude of 7. A magnitude of 8 is 10 x 10 x 10 (or 1,000) times a magnitude of 5.

The total amount of energy released by an earthquake increases even more rapidly than its strength. For instance, on the Richter scale, the energy released by a magnitude of 7 is thirty times greater than the energy released by a magnitude of 6.

Recent Earthquake Studies

New Madrid, Missouri, is not located along the border of two crustal plates. It is in a river valley in the center of the United States. What caused the violent earthquake that occurred there in 1811? Scientists didn't solve that mystery until the early 1970s.

At that time scientists began examining the subsurface structure of the Mississippi Valley. To do so, they used seismic profiling. In this method, tiny earthquakes are created. Sometimes small amounts of explosives are set off; sometimes machines release bursts of compressed air into the rock.

In the Mississippi Valley they also used special trucks equipped with powerful vibrating pads. These pads were lowered from the bottom of the moving trucks. They shook the ground like the pounding feet of a giant robot.

Charles Richter devised the earthquake-measuring scale that bears his name.

Scientists measured the speed of the seismic waves that resulted from these "miniquakes." The speed increased or decreased in varying types of rock or soil. The waves themselves produced one type of "signal" when they were passing through water. They gave out another type when they were passing through air. From these signals, scientists were able to obtain a map of the rock layers beneath the surface of the earth.

They found that the underground layers of rock were riddled with cracks. Great chunks of rock were broken and displaced. In some sections, entire rock layers had dropped as much as 3,000 feet (950 m) below their original positions. And there was a major fault line that zigzagged from Arkansas through Missouri and into southern Illinois.

The movements that created that fault probably took place about 300 million years ago. And the earth beneath the Mississippi River Valley is still on the move today.

Looking northward along the San Andreas Fault.

Currently, the most studied fault in the world is the San Andreas Fault in California. Parkfield, which is halfway between Los Angeles and San Francisco, is near the San Andreas Fault. Here, in some locations, the two sides of the fault are slipping smoothly past each other. In other locations, blocks of rock are sticking together. Stress builds up until there is a sudden lurch. Such lurches occurred in 1857, 1881, 1901, 1922, 1934, and 1966. The activity has occurred on an

Escarpments such as this one are formed when an earthquake causes a section of land to sink.

average of every twenty-two years, except in 1934, when it was ten years early.

Despite that one irregularity, this area appears to be the most predictable stretch of fault line in the world. Many researchers believe there will be another Parkfield earthquake before 1993. To monitor the seismic activity, the region is "really wired," as one seismologist said. Creepmeters measure earth movement by means of wires strung between points on opposite sides of the fault. Instruments that measure changes in pressure have been placed in deep wells. A laser precisely measures changes in the position of certain points on the earth's surface.

Seismologists know that rock has to bend before it breaks. At Parkfield, they are trying to measure that bending before the break happens. This knowledge may give them a valuable clue as to when an earthquake will occur not only in Parkfield, but in other places, too.

Seismologists Study the Past

When the earthquake struck, the mother fell to the floor. She held her baby tightly to her chest. The father threw himself over both of them. He was trying to protect them from the building blocks that were falling to the floor. Some of those blocks weighed 300 pounds (136 kg).

On the other side of the large house, a laborer took refuge in the doorway of his tiny room. The wall collapsed around him. He was killed almost instantly.

Not far from the house there was a stable. A teen-aged girl had been trying to calm a frightened mule. Both the girl and the animal died when the building toppled.

This earthquake occurred more than sixteen centuries ago on the island of Cyprus, near Greece. At the time, writers described it as "a frightful disaster, surpassing anything related either in legend or authentic history."

In 1934, J. F. Daniel, an archaeologist, was looking for evidence of an ancient civilization. He dug a trench on a bluff above a harbor on Cyprus. There he found the remains of an old Roman house in what had been the city of Kourion. The crumbled walls told him that the house had been destroyed by an earthquake.

In 1980, David Soren saw some coins that Daniel had found in the house. None of them were dated later than 365 A.D. That was the year the "frightful disaster" had struck the eastern Mediterranean area.

Soren was convinced that the house that Daniel had found had been destroyed in that particular earthquake. He uncovered the house room by room. He found the skeletons of the people who had died there. In another building, he found what must have been a marketplace. There were many animal bones in front of the marketplace. Inside was the skeleton of a man who was preparing to bake bread. In front of him were stones for grinding grain. Behind him was charred grain in a pot on a stove.

Soren spent several years digging on Cyprus. As he worked, he pieced together what must have happened on that dreadful day. It was just before 5 A.M., and the sun was rising. As many animals seem to do before an earthquake, the mule became nervous. The young girl heard him stamping about in his stall. She ran out to calm him. Moments later, the first shock hit. She fell to the ground and became entangled in the mule's flailing legs.

Meanwhile, walls shook and roofs collapsed. Most people were still in bed. They had time only to curl up and put their hands over their heads.

An even stronger shock quickly followed the first one. On the Mercalli scale, it would have measured IX or X. For 10 seconds, the ground shook like a mass of gelatin. Walls seemed to explode. Heavy objects flew through the air. A massive building crumpled, burying the "Daniel house" under tons of limestone blocks.

A third temblor struck soon after the first two. By this time, almost everyone in Kourion was either dead or dying.

Their bodies lay forgotten until J. F. Daniel and David Soren uncovered them. Soren said, "We felt like a rescue party arriving sixteen centuries too late."

3

Earthquake Country

Earthquake country has no boundaries, because the earth's crust is always moving. Usually, the movement is slow and gentle. Some of the tremors can't be detected even by a seismograph.

Every day, though, somewhere in the world, there is a movement that's strong enough to be felt by people. Such movement can occur anywhere, anytime. But almost all violent, destructive tremors occur in one of the two main earthquake zones.

Japan is located within in an earthquake zone called the Ring of Fire. In Tokyo, almost every day, tremors rattle cups on shelves, and floorboards creak. The people who live there pay little attention. They know that in three or four seconds, the earth will probably be still again. There will be little or no damage.

But sometimes the earthquakes are strong and destructive. On September 1, 1923, the earth rolled and pitched. Buildings were shaken off their foundations. Within 30 minutes, wind-whipped fires were burning all over the city. Firefighters could do nothing to stop them because the earthquake had broken all the water mains. By the end of the day, a hundred thousand people had been killed.

The people of southern Italy live within the Eurasian earthquake zone. In the spring of 1783, the ground shivered. The shivering became a wavelike motion. Soon, the ground was shaking violently. Sturdy buildings twisted and toppled. Thousands of people lost their lives.

Volcanoes and Earthquakes

Japan and Italy have both suffered many destructive earthquakes. They have also suffered from many volcanic eruptions. Frequently, an earthquake occurs at the same time as an eruption.

Like an earthquake, a volcanic eruption is the result of powerful underground forces. It begins when heavy layers of solid rock push down upon an underground pool of *magma*, or molten rock. As the magma is squeezed, it escapes sideway and upward into cracks and holes in the solid rock. The pressure causes the rock to swell, and more cracks appear. Sometimes great pieces of rock shift or are pushed aside by the magma. Seismic waves are set off.

The magma may melt through the layer of rock that surrounds it. Eventually, so much rock may be melted that a huge hole forms near the surface of the earth. This reservoir becomes a storage tank for the rising magma.

As more and more magma collects in the reservoir, it starts to push on the underside of the earth's surface. Some of the magma's gases are released. They expand, and pressure builds up. More seismic waves are set off.

When the gas pressure is strong enough, it pushes the magma up and out of the volcanic *vent*, or opening. As the volcano erupts, the mountain trembles. Cracks appear on its sides. Earthquakes are felt in the nearby countryside.

On September 29, 1955, the Soviet Union's Kamchatka Peninsula was struck by the first of hundreds of daily earthquakes. The epicenter of these temblors was near a volcano. The volcano had not erupted for so long it was thought to be *dormant*, or dead.

By October 22, the peninsula was experiencing more than 200 earthquakes daily. On that day, the volcano erupted. As it continued to spew gases, steam, and ashes, the number of earthquakes increased to 450 a day.

For a month, the eruptions continued and so did the earthquakes. Then, near the end of November, both the eruptions and the temblors declined. For four months, the volcano was still. But on March 30, 1956, there was a tremendous eruption of molten material. The blast destroyed the top 650 feet (200 m) of the mountain. It blew down trees that stood up to 15 miles (24 km) away. At the same time, a strong earthquake rocked the peninsula.

After that eruption, the magma sank back into the earth. There were more earthquakes as the rock settled and contracted. By June, the mountain and the earth were still.

Usually, the volcanic eruption causes the earthquake. Sometimes, though, an earthquake causes an eruption, On November 29, 1975, there was an earthquake near Mount Kilauea on the island of Hawaii. The magma in the reservoir was superhot and full of gas. It reacted to the shaking of the earth like carbonated water in a bottle that has been shaken. Bubbles of gas and steam erupted through the vent. Rivers of molten material flowed down the sides of the mountain to the sea.

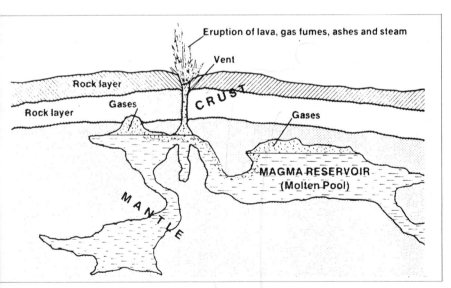

This cross-section of the earth's crust shows how magma pools come to the surface, causing volcanic eruptions.

The Ring of Fire

At one time, it was thought that volcanic eruptions were the cause of most earthquakes. Then, scientists studied the areas in which most temblors occur. They found that volcanoes are responsible for only a small number of earthquakes. Most are of tectonic origin, caused by the moving plates of the earth's crust.

All far-reaching earthquakes are of the tectonic variety. However, there is a lot of volcanic activity in both of the main earthquakes zones. The Ring of Fire was so named because of all the volcanoes that are located there.

Over three-fourths of all strong earthquakes occur in the Ring of Fire, which extends from Alaska down the coast of North America. In Central America, it bulges outward. It then turns back to continue down the South American coast to its southern tip in Antarctica. After crossing the Pacific Ocean, it continues to the Philippines, Japan, and the Kamchatka Peninsula.

A series of undersea trenches follows the same path as the Ring of Fire. These trenches are deeper than the height of the highest mountains on earth. It is within these trenches that oceanic plate slides under continental plate. The continental plate buckles and folds, like the hood of a car that strikes a wall. In this way, mountains such as the Andes were formed.

The meeting of the two plates creates much friction and heat. When the crustal material becomes hot enough to melt, a volcanic eruption may occur.

The meeting of two plates causes more than volcanic eruptions. It is inside the trenches that most of the world's destructive earthquakes are centered.

Chile is part of the Ring of Fire. Here, on May 21, 1960, in the morning darkness, a strong shock shook the peninsula of Arauco. Knowing there might be more shocks, the people left their homes and fled to open fields. Half-an-hour later, there was another shock. The next 33 hours were calm, and everyone began to relax.

Sunday, May 22, was a beautiful, balmy day. Most people were already outdoors when the shocks began again. At 3 o'clock that afternoon, rocks started to slip along an underwater fault just off the coast. The slippage caused an earthquake that was ten times greater than the first shock. All of the southern half of South America quivered. In and around Arauco, 60,000 homes became rubble within a few seconds. Dozens of larger buildings also crumbled and fell. Fortunately, it was Sunday, and the weather was pleasant. Had it been a weekday, or had rain been falling, most people would have been inside. When the structures collapsed, there would have been thousands of victims.

During the following week, three more sections of the undersea fault gave way. By then, the weather was cold and rainy, and most people were inside. Those tremors caused many deaths and injuries.

Much of the damage in this earthquake was caused by liquefaction. A car sank into soil that could no longer support any weight. Streams of liquefied soil flowed into the sea. Houses that had not been damaged by the temblors suddenly collapsed.

Liquefied soil poured into one harbor, causing a ship to become landlocked. Later, the owner turned the ship into a hotel.

The Eurasian Earthquake Zone

About 15 percent of all earthquakes take place in the Eurasian earthquake zone. This zone stretches in an east-west direction from Indonesia to the Mediterranean Sea region. It includes China, Iran, India, and the Middle East. In much of this area, two continental plates are colliding head-on. In Asia, one plate is traveling northward at the rate of 2 inches (5 cm) a year.

Soviet Armenia is located in the Eurasian earthquake zone. In December 1988, this country was shaken by an earthquake with a magnitude of 6.9. One bustling city and dozens of villages were reduced to rubble, while many others were almost completely destroyed. Over 40,000 people were killed when poorly designed buildings collapsed and buried them.

China has suffered from seismic activity more than any other country in the world. It is estimated that altogether 13,000,000 Chinese have been killed in earthquakes. The 1556 Shensi disaster claimed 830,000 victims. In 1920 in Kansu Province, 180,000 people died. The survivors told of mountains that walked. They recalled seeing hills 100 feet (30 m) high being pushed up out of flat land.

In one instance, a quarter-mile section of road and the trees that bordered it were moved 4,800 feet (1,500 m). And a house with two people in it was carried a half-mile (0.8 km) down a mountain. It was then moved another half-mile into a valley.

Just twelve years later, Kansu was hit by another earthquake that killed 70,000 more people.

Portugal lies on the other end of the Eurasian seismic zone. In 1755, its capital, Lisbon, was the center of a worldwide empire. The morning of Saturday, November 1 of that year, was clear and still. It was All Saint's Day, so many of the city's quarter-million people were in church.

At 9:40 A.M., the city suddenly shuddered violently. There was a roar that sounded like thunder. Church steeples waved to and fro. The buildings themselves rocked back and forth, then up and down. The terrified worshippers rushed outside and huddled in the square. Plaster and bricks broke loose from the walls of the buildings around them. Everyone who was standing there was crushed by the shower of falling objects.

Meanwhile, throughout the city, buildings collapsed into the narrow streets. Hundreds of people fled to a nearby river. Many of them stood on a wide wall along the waterfront, but the soft earth beneath the wall gave way and the wall crashed into the river. Many more people were drowned when a 50-foot (15-m) wave of water swept over the beach and washed a half-mile (0.8 km) inland. More than 60,000 lives were lost that morning. The survivors had to flee fires that burned for more than three days.

This building, along with many others, was destroyed by a 1908 earthquake in Messina, Italy.

People all over Europe felt the shocks from the Lisbon earthquake. In North Africa, some soldiers were killed when their barracks collapsed. Altogether the tremors traveled throughout an area of 1,000,000 square miles (2,600,000 square km).

Earthquake Country in North America

Canada is not generally thought of as being earthquake country. However, some temblors in the southeastern part of that country have been quite strong. One, which occurred in Quebec in 1663, was recorded by Jesuit missionaries. From their description, it may have been as violent as the 1811 New Madrid earthquake. Fortunately, there weren't many people living in the area at that time.

On the morning of September 19, 1985, an earthquake of 8.1 magnitude struck Mexico City. In the downtown section, more than 100 buildings collapsed, and many more were damaged beyond repair. The next day a strong aftershock caused still more destruction. Twenty thousand people died as a result of that catastrophe.

In the United States, California is the state that most people think of as earthquake country. On July 21, 1952, the city of Bakersfield was struck by an earthquake that was felt all over southern California. The 1971 San Fernando Valley earthquake killed 64 people, injured 2,400, and caused a half-billion dollars worth of damage. In October 1987, another earthquake in the Los Angeles area tumbled buildings and walls.

Southern California suffers more than its share of quakes. But in October 1989, it was northern California that experienced the worst United States earthquake since 1906. As in that earlier disaster, it was the area in and around San Francisco that was struck. The earthquake, which measured 6.9 on the Richter scale, caused the top portion of a double-deck freeway to collapse onto a lower portion. It was here that most of the 59 fatalities occurred.

This earthquake took place as thousands of people were crowding into San Francisco's Candlestick Park for the third game of the World

Series. Fortunately, the seating structures did not collapse, and the people did not panic. If they had, the casualty toll would have been much higher.

But California isn't the only state that has a history of seismic activity. Alaska has had some of the worst earthquakes of this century. Along the southern Alaskan coast, a continental plate meets an oceanic plate.

The most famous Alaskan earthquake is the Good Friday disaster of 1964. That temblor was centered on the Denali Fault near Anchorage and Valdez. At 5:26 A.M., the earth quivered and trembled. The shaking lasted less than a minute, but when it was over much of Anchorage had become rubble. Its main street was a series of cliffs, some more than 10 feet (3 m) high. The sagging earth had taken entire sections of the city with it. The control tower at the airport was destroyed. The tsunami, a huge wave, that followed the earthquake was worse. Traveling at 200 miles (320 km) an hour, it came ashore as a mammoth breaker. Towns all along the coast were wiped out.

A survivor of the 1917 San Salvador earthquake examines the ruins of a public building.

On August 31, 1886, Charleston, South Carolina, suffered an earthquake almost as strong as the one in New Madrid. Large cracks appeared in the ground, railroad ties were split and twisted, and tremors were felt over an area of 3,000,000 square miles (7,770,000 square km). South Carolina is not considered to be part of an earthquake zone. Nevertheless, each year there are several slight to moderate earthquakes. Studies have shown the seismic activity is a result of hundreds of deep, ancient fault lines.

The states of Washington and Oregon are more famous for their volcanic eruptions than for their seismic activity, but Puget Sound has a moderate earthquake about every six months. Many scientists believe that someday one of these states will suffer a strong, very destructive earthquake.

In Utah's Wasatch Mountains, earthquakes are common. There

This freeway overpass collapsed during the San Fernando earthquake.

are many dams, and if the tremors ever cause a dam to fail, thousands of people could drown.

The New England states have a long history of earth tremors. Many of the cities and towns of southern New England are built upon sand and gravel, and a strong earthquake would probably destroy many of them. There would be less damage in Maine. Here, the cities are constructed upon solid rock.

Missouri lies on a great fault that divides the United States in half. It was the site of the 1811 New Madrid catastrophe. Scientists think that someday it may suffer another violent earthquake. This region is now the center of a large chemical industry. Many of these chemicals are fatal to human beings and to animals, and an earthquake could cause chemical spills that would take thousands of lives.

Alaska was devastated by an earthquake in 1964.

4

The Killer Waves

On a June day in 1896, the residents of a Japanese coastal city were celebrating a festival. The streets were crowded with laughing men, women, and children. On the beach, strolling people were enjoying the pleasant weather. The warm waters of the Pacific Ocean sparkled under the sun and wavelets danced along the shore.

About 7 P.M., the merrymakers felt the ground roll beneath their feet. The first earth movement was soon followed by several minor aftershocks. The people paused briefly in their conversation and laughter, but then continued as though nothing had happened. They were used to mild earth tremors.

Twenty minutes after the first shock, there was a sound like the patter of rain on the sea. The sound grew into a roar, then there was a sudden silence. The ocean was as smooth as glass. The people were quiet.

Suddenly, the roar returned, and a 70-foot (21-m) -high wall of water bore down upon the coast. The terrified people ran toward the hills, but it was too late for 25,000 of them. They had become the victims of a tsunami, a killer wave.

Beneath the Surface of the Sea

Many people who survived an earthquake were later killed by a tsunami. What causes a tsunami? The answer to that question lies beneath the surface of the sea.

There was a time when everyone thought that the ocean floor was a dead, unchanging place. We now know that the truth is just the opposite. The seafloor is constantly active, always changing.

Here and there, dotting the flatlands of the seafloor, there are hot spots. In these areas, there are volcanoes that occasionally erupt. The Hawaiian Islands are located directly above one of these hot spots. The islands themselves were formed from ancient volcanoes that rose from the seafloor.

Towering over these isolated volcanoes, is the midocean ridge, an undersea mountain range. Its peaks are as raw and ragged as a shark's teeth. Its mountains are as high above their base as the Rockies or the Alps.

The section that winds down from the Arctic, southward through the Atlantic Ocean and around Africa, is the Mid-Atlantic Ridge. The

The tremendous force of a tsunami almost demolished this seaport warehouse in Seward, Alaska.

section that is located in the Indian Ocean is called the Carlsberg Ridge. The East Pacific Rise moves east to pass Australia on the south. Then, swinging north, it runs parallel to the western coast of South America.

With a length of 40,000 miles (64,000 km), the entire midocean ridge is long enough to wrap twice around the earth. It is, in fact, the largest single geologic formation on our planet.

A steep-walled valley, or rift, runs down the middle of much of the ridge. Within this rift, sections of oceanic plate are drifting apart. Some parts of the rift seem to be located above hot spots in the ocean floor.

The hot spots are caused by convection currents that rise and bring heat from the bottom of the mantle. The currents carry molten material to the surface of the seafloor. The heat and the pressure from this material cause the surrounding seafloor to swell. Eventually, it swells so much that *fissures*, or cracks, appear.

Sometimes great blocks of the seafloor break off and tumble into the fissures. There are frequent landslides on the sloping sides of the rift, and there are many earthquakes.

There is also a lot of activity in the submarine trenches that border the Atlantic, Pacific, and Indian oceans. Here, billions of tons of rock are smashed together by terrific forces. Here, we have learned, many volcanic eruptions have their beginnings. Here, too, many tsunamis are born.

What Is a Tsunami?

A tsunami begins when there is an abrupt movement on the ocean floor. Perhaps there is some volcanic activity. Perhaps an earthquake causes the seafloor to heave and plunge. Perhaps a great fissure opens up, and there is an undersea landslide.

Any violent undersea activity can act like a giant paddle that whacks the surrounding water and sets it into motion. The greater the jolt, or whack, the greater the volume of water that is moved. Often, millions of tons of water are displaced. This mass of water, moving toward the surface of the ocean, shoves the layers of water above it. Still more water is added to the fast-growing mass.

The wave quickly reaches the ocean's surface. It pushes out on all sides, making a huge mound. The mound levels out into a series of broad, shallow waves. One by one, the waves start their journey across the ocean. They can travel at speeds up to 600 miles (1,000 km) an hour.

On the open sea, the crest of these waves, or tsunamis, may be only 2 to 3 feet (0.6 to 0.9 m) high. The waves in the series may be from 100 to 400 miles (160 to 640 km) apart. As a result, the crew on a ship in the middle of the ocean would feel only the swell of normal water movement. Often, the tsunami runs out of energy before reaching a shore. Then it causes no damage.

But some tsunamis remain strong. When one nears a shore, the shallower ocean floor drags on the wave and the wave loses its bottom layer of water. To make up for the loss, the wave may inhale the coastal water like a giant vacuum cleaner. Meanwhile, the back part of the wave rushes forward at tremendous speed. It piles up behind the forward part. Within minutes a 3-foot (0.9-m) swell may grow to a terrifying height of 50 feet (15 m). By the time it reaches the beach, it may be two or three times higher.

This killer wave breaks on the shore and crashes over the land, smashing buildings and boats. Within minutes, the first wave may be followed by a second, possibly a third, and even a fourth and fifth. The waves then taper off, but several days may pass before the sea is normal again.

Not all tsunamis are mammoth waves that travel thousands of miles. There are many undersea fault zones along the coast of California. Mild earthquakes often cause these faults to quiver, and undersea landslides are common. When a large piece of rock breaks loose at the top of a fault, it leaves a hole. The hole creates suction that pulls at the surface of the ocean, and the disturbance can send a small tsunami rolling toward shore.

Another tsunami may be created when a piece of rock shifts position at the bottom of a fissure, or fault. The wave that results may not be strong enough to cause any damage on shore, but the force of several waves coming together could create breakers that pound piers and wash over highways.

Krakatoa

Krakatoa is a small island in the Sunda Straits of Indonesia. Before 1883, hardly anyone except sailors in passing ships and the residents of nearby Java and Sumatra had ever heard of it.

In the early spring of that year, steam and dust began rising from Rakata, one of the three volcanoes on the island. A few weeks later, people living near the straits felt the earth tremble. By May, the volcano's mutterings had changed to roars, but no one was worried. In that part of the world, such activity is considered normal.

On August 26, however, the volcano's warnings could no longer be ignored. Steam rose to a height of 700 feet (200 m). Every 10 minutes there was an explosion, some of which shook houses hundreds of miles (several hundred km) away. Cracks appeared on the sides of the mountain.

At dawn the next day, the sides of the volcano burst open. There

This boat was tossed ashore at Seward, Alaska by the March 1964 tsunami.

38

was a deafening explosion. A little after 10 o'clock that morning, there was another mammoth explosion. Five cubic miles (20.8 cubic km) of rock and dirt were blown out of the inside of the volcano. There wasn't enough material left to support the peak. It collapsed into the volcano. As it fell, it carried two-thirds of the island with it.

Millions of gallons (or liters) of water rushed to fill the hole that was left when the island sank. The water mixed with molten volcanic material. There was a final tremendous explosion.

By then, everyone in the area was trembling with fright. They would have been even more frightened had they known that the worst was yet to come. The ocean had been greatly disturbed by all of the activity, and a tsunami was formed. It raced away from Krakatoa at speeds up to 350 miles (560 km) an hour. Approaching land, it grew higher and stronger. It was as high as a 12-story building when it crashed down upon the coast of Java. Within minutes, it destroyed 300 villages, and parts of Sumatra were covered with 80 feet (24 m) of water.

People in the path of the tsunami had no time to escape. They had no place to hide. The wave swept across the low-lying islands, carrying everything with it. Ships were torn from their moorings; some were later found many miles (or km) inland.

The force of the tsunami was felt many thousands of miles (or km) away. The water in South African ports rose and fell, causing ships to tug at their anchors.

Krakatoa is still remembered as the scene of a tremendous volcanic eruption. But it was not the eruption that did the damage. It was the resulting tsunami that destroyed millions of dollars worth of property. It was the killer wave that took 36,000 human lives.

Predicting Tsunamis

It was April Fool's day of 1946. The people on the beach at Hilo, Hawaii, barely noticed a slightly larger-than-average wave breaking at their feet. They were puzzled, though, when the water pulled back much further than usual. Coral reefs were exposed, and stranded fish flapped on the sand.

Many curious people walked out to take a closer look. A few minutes later, they were drowned by a monster wave that crashed upon the beach.

The 1946 Hilo tsunami wrecked bridges, railroad tracks, and highways. It demolished homes and other buildings and washed away entire stretches of beach. One hundred and seventy people were killed because of an earthquake that had occurred in far-off Alaska.

This disaster had one benefit, however. It resulted in the creation of the Tsunami Warning System. The system's nerve center is in Honolulu, where men and women keep a constant vigil, using computers, teletypewriters, and communications satellites.

Special instruments record traces of undersea earthquake activity. An oceanwide network of float gauges and pressure gauges measures passing waves. Its messages are sent to recording instruments. Ordinary tides, currents, and waves produce gentle, billowy lines. In contrast, tsunamis produce sharply peaked up-and-down lines.

When a tsunami threatens, a warning is sent to all the places that could be in danger. These warnings are often received in Alaska and in Chile, in the Fiji Islands, and in Hong Kong and New Zealand. Early on the morning of May 22, 1960, several cities in Hawaii were warned about a 400-mile (640-km)-an-hour tsunami headed their way. Many people paid no attention because there had recently been several such warnings, and no tsunamis had reached their island.

This time, though, everyone should have paid attention. The estimated time of arrival of the tsunami was correct to within one minute. At 9:58 A.M., the first wave hit the beach at Hilo. It was only four feet (1 m) high, but the second was 9 feet (3 m) high. The third was 35 feet (11 m) high. It swept away buildings and wiped out the city's power, transportation, and communication systems. More than 400 cars were crushed as if they were tin cans. Some were bent around trees until their front and rear bumpers joined.

Because the warning was so widely ignored, 61 people were killed.

After its destruction in Hilo, the tsunami swept on toward Japan. Although people there were also warned. they did nothing to protect themselves. The earthquake that created the tsunami had occurred in Chile, which is far from Japan. Almost everyone thought that the wave would be only a ripple by the time it reached their country.

Eight hours after it left Hawaii, a 12-foot (4-m) wave washed over the Japanese islands of Honshu and Hokkaido. With swift fury, it destroyed thousands of structures and killed 180 people.

On November 4, 1951, the people of Honolulu were warned about an approaching tsunami. In contrast to the people in Hilo and in Japan, they used sandbags and other objects to protect their homes and places of business. They then fled to high ground. As a result, there were no deaths and relatively little property damage.

Unlike earthquakes, tsunamis can be accurately predicted. When everyone starts paying attention to the warnings, the killer waves will claim no more victims.

5

Preparing for Disaster

Someday, scientists may be able to tell us the time and place that an earthquake will occur. Someday, scientists may be even be able to prevent an earthquake. Or they may be able to direct an earthquake away from a populated area.

Meanwhile, the best way to keep from becoming an earthquake victim is not to live in an earthquake zone. But what about the many millions of people who *do* live in such zones? The only way they can protect their lives and property is to be prepared for a disaster.

Many people are involved in earthquake preparedness programs. Architects and engineers are making buildings safer. Geologists are warning people not to build on unsafe ground. Schoolteachers are giving earthquake drills to their students. Civic groups are teaching people what to do in case of an earthquake.

But there is a big problem. Even in such places as southern California, many people don't pay attention to the warnings. "No one knows when an earthquake will occur," they say. "No one really knows *where* it will occur. It probably won't happen to me."

One thing is certain, though. In earthquake country, somewhere, sometime, the ground will start to roll and shake and crack open. And

unless the people who live there are ready, many lives will be lost that
could have been saved.

A Bitter Lesson

It was Saturday, September 1, 1923. In the Japanese cities of Tokyo
and Yokohama, a seaport 17 miles (27 km) to the south, shops and
offices were closing for the weekend. Crowds were gathering at
seashore resorts. Tokyo's new Imperial Hotel was about to open with
a gala luncheon celebration. It had been especially designed to resist
earthquake damage.

Just before noon, a savage earthquake shook the two cities for
almost five minutes. Shortly thereafter, a murderous tsunami 36 feet
(11 m) in height, lashed the coast.

Wooden buildings usually withstand earthquakes, but more than
12,000 of Yokohama's 100,000 wooden houses were splintered. Red-
hot coals from hundreds of overturned stoves set the wreckage on fire.

In Tokyo, a twelve-story building swayed and broke apart at the
eighth floor. But most of the damage occurred in the older part of town,
where houses were built upon swampy soil. Here, as in Yokohama,
fire caused more damage than the earthquake itself. The separate fires
formed two massive fronts. They roared toward each other.

Great crowds of panicked people gathered in the narrow streets of
the cities and ran toward the river in search of safety. As they started
across the various bridges, the crowds from each city ran into each
other. The people couldn't go forward. They couldn't go back.

Soon, the two walls of fire reached the river. Falling cinders ignited
the bridges. Thousands of people died in the flames.

The Imperial Hotel survived the disaster with only slight damage.
The success of its design proved that earthquakes need not level
buildings. Government officials decided to prevent future deaths by
rebuilding Tokyo and Yokohoma with earthquake-resistant structures.
There would be no more narrow, twisted streets. Instead, there would

be broad avenues that could not become blocked by rubble. The avenues would also act as firebreaks.

Since so many wooden homes had been destroyed by the earthquake and the fires, the replacements would be made of concrete.

These plans were never carried out. Even as they were being made, people were building houses from packing cases and old boards. Many residents left town to live with relatives in the country, and there were not enough workers left to rebuild the cities according to the new plans.

What Has Been Learned

Perhaps it was just as well that Tokyo and Yokohama weren't rebuilt at that time. It was later found that concrete buildings often collapse during an earthquake. What *are* the most earthquake-resistant building materials? And what are the best methods of construction?

To find the answers to those questions, the engineers examined the construction of the Imperial Hotel. They took close looks at other buildings that had survived earthquakes. They studied the up-and-down (vertical) and sidewise (horizontal) ground motions of many earthquakes. Then, in the early 1940s, they built a shaking table. Using this table, they could see how model buildings hold up during the twisting, shifting, bouncing, whiplash movements that occur during a real earthquake.

In 1974, Japanese and U.S. scientists designed an earthquake computer program. The program included information about different seismic areas. Is the soil loose or hard? How many earthquakes have occurred there? How often do they occur? What are the known tectonic forces in the region?

They gave the answers to those questions to architects and engineers. Now, earthquake-resistant structures could be designed for a particular location.

The value of earthquake-resistant buildings can be shown by contrasting the death tolls in the 1988 earthquake in Soviet Armenia and the 1989 San Francisco earthquake. These earthquakes had about the same magnitude, but in Soviet Armenia, none of the buildings were earthquake resistant. As a result, many thousands of people were killed and injured. In San Francisco, older buildings built on unstable soil collapsed. But the newer buildings, which were earthquake resistant, survived the tremors. As a result, thousands of lives were probably saved.

Buildings aren't the only things that have to be made earthquake-resistant, however. Gas and water pipes and telephone lines must also be protected. California has done a great deal to protect its water system. Alaska's main electrical plants automatically shut down when the ground begins to tremble, and its major gas lines are shut off when there are sudden changes in pressure in the pipes.

Tokyo has used engineering to build earthquake-resistant structures. Its officials have also done much to ease the day-to-day effect of an earthquake. They have stored 400,000 tons of water—a ten-day supply—in underground cisterns and earthquake-resistant warehouses. They have stored blankets and food for the city's 12 million residents. More than a hundred parks and open spaces are designed as evacuation areas and the roads leading to them are plainly marked. There are fire extinguishers in boxes along the main streets.

Many business people are also prepared for disaster. Most of the city's taxicabs are equipped with fire extinguishers. Some of the larger companies store rice and bottled water for their workers. One large office building has forty water cannons on its roof.

All of Tokyo's citizens know what to do during and after an earthquake. In their homes, they have survival kits that contain a flashlight, a fire extinguisher, first-aid supplies, and a transistor radio. Each family has enough food and water for two or three days.

Japanese seismologists are constantly on the lookout for signs of a coming earthquake. If they believe a strong one is on the way, the alarm is sounded on radio and television. Loudspeakers announce it in the streets. Sirens and bells are sounded. Emergency teams rush to their posts. Factory workers turn off their machines. Office workers take safe positions in their buildings. People at home turn off their gas and electricity. They pick up their survival kits and go to evacuation areas.

Other countries are also making preparations for earthquakes. In Iran, flat-roofed adobe houses are being replaced by reinforced-brick structures. In the Soviet Union, subways with earthquake-resistant connectors between the tunnel sections are being built. In Los Angeles, all new high-rise buildings must be earthquake-resistant and must have sprinkler systems to put out fires.

Earthquake Engineering

Today, in earthquake country, engineers and seismologists are working together to build earthquake-resistant buildings, bridges, and freeway overpasses. They know the danger of building upon certain types of soil. In the 1960 Chilean earthquake, buildings near the beach moved in every direction. In an earthquake in Niigata, Japan, in 1964, entire apartment buildings tipped over. Still in one piece, they seemed to be floating on top of the ground. In both places the loose, sandy soil had become soaked with water.

This building contains the housing control room of the Space Flight Operations Center, NASA Deep Space Network, Jet Propulsion Laboratory. It was found after construction that it is located on a fault line. Fortunately it is an earthquake-resistant structure.

Today, there is much concern about building nuclear power plants on such soil. One solution would be to replace the sand with denser material. Another would be to carry the building's foundation far below the ground's surface. Many engineers believe it would be better not to build at all at such locations.

Why do some buildings survive an earthquake while others that are similar do not? Engineers asked that question after an earthquake in Venezuela. The trembling had caused severe damage in one part of Caracas, but just a few blocks away there was only a little damage. It was later found that the two areas had different types of soil.

Another concern is building in areas that have a history of landslides. In mountainous country, earthquakes have caused landslides that have buried entire towns. During one Chilean earthquake, terrified people ran from the coast to high ground to escape a tsunami. They were later swept into the sea by great rivers of mud.

Engineers have also learned the dangers of building on filled land, where earth has been dumped over swamps and into ravines. The worst damage in the 1906 San Francisco earthquake occurred in parts of the city that had been built on filled land. Since that time, it has been proved again and again that earthquakes need not be killers. Most people die because flimsy structures have been built on loose soil.

Year after year, more is being learned about how to prepare for a violent earthquake. Japan leads the world in earthquake preparedness. The people who live there face a day-to-day danger.

Californians, on the other hand, know there will eventually be a big earthquake but they do little to get ready for it. They build roads and pipelines across the San Andreas Fault. They build hundreds of houses, factories, and schools near the fault. They even build hospitals where there is great danger of an earthquake.

More than 18 million people live and work near the San Andreas Fault. They can see for themselves how rows of trees have been offset by as much as 10 feet (3 m). They can see sections of drainage ditches that have been cracked and moved a half-inch (0.10 cm) a year. Many ocean-front homes built on unstable cliffs will almost certainly fall into the water during a strong quake.

How Your Family Can Prepare for an Earthquake

No one should depend entirely on government officials and engineers for earthquake protection. Each person and each family can do a lot to prepare for a possible disaster. Here are some ideas.

1. Store enough bottled water and canned or dried foods to last forty-eight hours. Don't forget food for your pets.
2. Keep sturdy shoes and a flashlight beside each bed.
3. Keep a battery-operated radio and extra batteries on hand.
4. Have a first-aid kit in your home and car.
5. Place beds away from large windows.
6. Keep doors and hallways clear of obstacles.
7. Strap bookcases and hot-water heaters to a wall.
8. Know the locations of the electrical fuse box and the shut-off valves for gas and water. Learn how to turn them off.
9. Discuss what would happen in each room of your house if there were a real earthquake. In the kitchen, would cupboard doors fly open, letting dishes and glasses tumble out and shatter? Would the refrigerator slide across the floor or fall over? In the den, would books fly off bookshelves? In the front room, is there a heavy wall ornament that could become a flying missile? In the dining room, is there a chandelier or a loose ceiling fixture that could fall? In the bedrooms, are there headboards full of books and other objects that could strike a sleeping person?
10. Now get rid of those hazards. Tie cupboard doors. Strap books onto shelves or lower the shelves. Secure any heavy wall hanging. Move beds to safe positions.

If an earthquake strikes, you will have only seconds to protect yourself. A simple game will help you to react quickly.

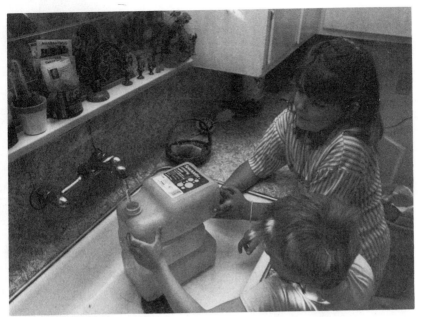

The stored emergency water supply should be changed every six months. A few drops of liquid bleach helps to keep bottled water fresh.

Taking shelter under a sturdy table may save your life during an earthquake.

The game starts when any member of the family shouts "Earthquake!" At that time, you and everyone else in the house must pretend that a real earthquake has struck. Remember that you have only a second or two to react. If the floor is moving a great deal, you may be able to move only a short distance. Take shelter under a nearby table. Stand in a doorway. Crouch in a corner. If you are in bed, put a pillow over your head.

During a real earthquake, remain in your safe position until the rolling and shaking stops. Then go outside. Stand away from walls and windows. Stay calm.

Don't use the telephone unless you need help right away.

If you smell leaking gas, turn the gas shut-off valve to the off position. If water mains are damaged, shut off the main valve. If electrical appliances are wet, turn off the electricity.

Listen to a radio for information and official instructions.

Earthquakes can't be prevented. But preparation can do a lot to prevent injury. It can even save your life.

Knowing how to turn off the main gas line may prevent a fire or an explosion.

6

Predicting Earthquakes

Many of nature's warning signals are easily understood. The rumbling of a volcano tells people there may be an eruption within days or weeks. A tornado's funnel-shaped cloud can be seen when it is still several miles (or km) away. People in its path have time to take shelter.

Weather forecasters can predict what day a hurricane will strike a seacoast. Many lives will be saved if people leave the area.

But earthquakes seem to give no warning at all. One minute the ground is solid and secure, the next minute it is rolling and shaking.

Some seismologists, however, believe that earthquakes *do* send out warnings. There have been times when these warnings have appeared to be strong and clear. More often, they are vague and confusing, because the science of earthquake prediction is new.

It is hoped that within the next five to ten years, scientists will find better ways to understand the signals that come before an earthquake. If they do, they will know when and where a temblor will strike. They may even know how strong it will be. They will be able to warn people of the coming event.

If people heed that warning, they can protect themselves. Accurate earthquake prediction could save hundreds of thousands of lives.

An Earthquake's Warning Signals

China, the Soviet Union, Japan, and the United States have all suffered disastrous earthquakes. These countries have a special interest in finding a way to forecast an earthquake.

Scientists believe that one of the signals may be a gradual tilting or bulging of a section of land. This movement occurs when the rock along a fault is being squeezed. As it is squeezed, it develops many small cracks. The pressure applied to the rock grows, and the cracks become larger. The rock expands. Eventually, it pushes upward. It may push the ground sidewise, or it may lift it up.

In 1958, a section of land near Niigata, Japan began to bulge. Within a year, there was a 2-inch (5-cm) bubble rising above the surface of the earth. Six years later, a major earthquake destroyed most of the city. Its epicenter was located at the highest point of the bulge.

Soviet scientists predicted a moderate temblor in Siberia by using

This deep crack in the road was caused by an earthquake that occurred in Three Forks, Montana in July 1925.

another signal. The ground there had become a better conductor of electricity, and this had happened before other earthquakes. Scientists believe it is caused by groundwater seeping into new cracks in the rocks. The water allows electricity to flow through the surface crust more quickly and easily than usual.

The Chinese have seen that just before an earthquake the water in deep wells may move upward or downward. The temperature of the water changes, too. And there may be more radon in the well water. *Radon* is a radioactive gas that is created by the decay of radium. The water that fills the cracks in the rocks carries radon from lower levels of the earth's crust.

By accident, it was discovered that water seeping into rocks is not only the *result* of seismic activity. This seepage can also be the *cause* of such activity. In 1961, U.S. Army engineers drilled a deep hole east of Denver, Colorado. Every few weeks they got rid of toxic waste water by pouring it into this hole. Three years later, geologists reported that there had been 710 earth tremors in the area around the hole.

The engineers stopped dumping the water, and the tremors became much less frequent. Geologists later reasoned that the increased water pressure had caused the rocks along the fault lines to break apart more easily. As they broke, their tension was released and seismic waves were set off.

In the early 1960s, scientists in the Soviet Union were studying sound waves that pass through the earth's crust. They found that these waves slowed down for months or years before an earthquake. Just before the earthquake, the velocity of the sound waves returned to normal.

In 1971, there was a destructive earthquake in California's San Fernando Valley. Afterward, seismologists looked at the records of the sound waves in the area. They saw that the sound waves had been slower than usual for three-and-a-half years before the earthquake.

The Chinese have noticed that zoo animals may become anxious just before an earthquake. Rats leave their holes and stagger around.

Fish thrash about in ponds. Dogs whine for no reason. So far, though, no one can prove that such unusual actions forecast an earthquake.

A Successful Prediction

Many of China's one billion people live in mud-brick, tile-roofed houses. Building materials are scarce, and they must use what's available. But these dwellings are almost certain to collapse during even a moderate temblor. Thus, many Chinese are in great danger of being killed in an earthquake.

In 1949, the Chinese government became determined to prevent this loss of life. One hundred thousand people were appointed amateur earthquake watchers. Every day, students, farmers, and factory workers observed animal behavior, water levels, and slight ground tremors.

In early 1975, in Liaoning Province, there were several signs that a major earthquake might be coming. Much of the region had been uplifted and tilted. Minor tremors were being felt five times more often than usual. The water in wells was bubbling. The water in ponds was

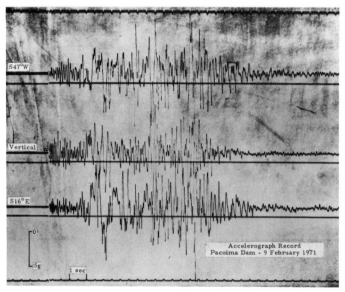

These tracings are a record of movements during an earthquake near Los Angeles, California in 1971.

muddy and had a strong odor. Snakes left their warm places of hibernation and lay frozen on icy roads.

On February 3, government officials said there would be a major earthquake within forty-eight hours. "Stay outside your homes," they told the people. Despite the cold weather, hundreds of thousands of people slept outside.

The next day, there were more tremors, then a strong jolt. "There will be a strong earthquake tonight," radio broadcasters warned that afternoon. Housewives put out their cooking fires. Farmers led their livestock from barns to open fields. Homes and shops were closed. As darkness fell, everyone sat shivering in tents and straw shelters.

The earthquake roared in at 7:36 that evening. The ground heaved. Sheets of light flashed across the sky. Roads buckled and bridges twisted. Fifteen-foot (5-m)-high jets of water and sand shot into the air. In one town, almost all of the buildings were destroyed. In all, 300 people were killed. Without the prediction, the number killed could have been 10,000.

The success of that prediction excited seismologists all over the world. Since then, the Chinese claim to have predicted at least ten other strong earthquakes. In the spring of 1976, however, they forecast an earthquake and hundreds of people slept in tents for two months. Then the signs of a coming temblor became vague and scattered. The officials said there had been a mistake. The people moved back into their homes.

Then, on July 28, the ground shook so hard that people were thrown to their ceilings. "It was like an ocean," said one survivor. "Everything was moving."

Scientists have had other problems with earthquake prediction. In 1958, in the desert area of southern California, a section of land started to rise. Seismologists watched the "Palmdale bulge" as it rose over a half-inch (0.10 cm) a year. But there was no earthquake. Instead, after several years, the bulge began to shrink.

There continue to be disappointments and difficulties in predicting earthquakes. But scientists will keep studying the signals that come from the earth. The more they learn, the better the chance of eventual success.

The Danger of a False Prediction

The Chinese have had some success in predicting major earthquakes. Geologists in the United States have been able to forecast some minor ones. In 1970, a geologist in the Soviet Union said that within ten years, there would be a good earthquake prediction system. But there is not yet such a system.

Prediction is difficult because every earthquake is different. Many "sure" signs are not sure at all. They may or may not occur right before an earthquake. As a result, government officials have a problem. Suppose the signs show that an earthquake might be coming. What should they do to prepare for it? What should they say to the people who will be affected?

Imagine, for example, there is a prediction of an earthquake of a magnitude of 8 in Los Angeles, California, sometime during the next few months. Some of the preparations would be simple. People would be told to store food, water, and medical supplies for their families. City officials could also store supplies in schools, warehouses, and hospitals. They could tell people what to do during and after the earthquake. Teams of people could be trained in rescue and in first aid.

Other preparations would not be so simple. Dams should be strengthened or emptied to prevent floods. The water level in reservoirs should be kept low. Poorly built public buildings should be reinforced. Very weak structures may have to be torn down.

Still more steps would have to be taken if the earthquake's warnings signs grew stronger. Officials might decide to shut down factories that make toxic chemicals and other dangerous substances. Trucks and trains that carry dangerous cargo would be kept away from the city. Nuclear power plants would be shut down.

When the earthquake is believed to be only weeks or days away, people might be encouraged to leave the city. No one would be allowed to enter. Bridges and freeway overpasses might be closed to traffic. Medical and rescue teams would be standing by to help in an emergency.

Just before the earthquake, all businesses would be shut down. Gas and electricity would be turned off. Anyone remaining in the area would be sleeping in parks and fields. The city's normal routine would come to a halt. And if the earthquake came, many thousands of lives would have been saved.

But what if the earthquake *didn't* come? Thousands of people would have lost time from work. Tourists would have stayed away. Everyone's life would have been disrupted. People might be angry at the scientists and the government officials. The next time there was a prediction, they might not pay any attention. And that might be the time when the earthquake *does* occur.

It is hoped that someday earthquake prediction will be more dependable. Until then, people may suffer because of a false alarm. But they will suffer even more if they are not prepared for a catastrophe.

The Research Continues

After the 1964 Alaska earthquake, the United States became very serious abut earthquake prediction. Monitoring systems were set up in many areas that were known to be seismically active. The first successful prediction took place in 1973 in the Adirondack Mountains region of New York.

There was another successful prediction in November 1974 near Hollister, California. Hollister is located on the San Andreas Fault. Here, the instruments measured changes in the earth's magnetic field. They measured a tilting of a section of land. They showed that there were slight shifts in the land along surveyed lines.

By November 27, the seismologists were almost certain there would soon be an earthquake. But they were worried about what would happen if they told the city's residents. The warning might cause some of them to panic. Panic makes people do foolish things.

No warning was given, and the next day Hollister was rocked by a moderate earthquake. Fortunately, the temblor lasted only a second or two and did no real damage.

Seismologists pay a lot of attention to two sections of the San Andreas fault. One is the section near San Francisco. Long before the 1989 San Francisco earthquake, there was concern about the small amount of seismic activity in that area. This lack of earth movement meant that stress was building up along the fault line. This stress was only partially relieved by the 6.9 tremor. According to the signs of earthquake prediction, the "Big One" might still be in northern California's near furture.

The other section being studied is near Los Angeles. Here, during the last few years, there have been several earthquakes. The epicenter of one of the strongest, on October 1, 1987, was 50 miles (80 km)

Using backpack-mounted equipment, this student is studying small earthquakes in Chile.

southeast of Los Angeles. It caused seven deaths and millions of dollars worth of damage.

Seismologists believe that there will be an earthquake of a magnitude of 8 somewhere along the southern San Andreas Fault within the next 30 to 50 years. It could cause 23,000 deaths and destroy $70 billion dollars worth of property. An accurate prediction would lessen the loss of life and prevent much damage.

Seismologists all over the world are using many methods to try to predict earthquakes. They record the number and sizes of earthquakes that have occurred in different areas. What has happened in the past gives them a good idea of what could happen in the future. The Chinese have been keeping seismic records for 2,000 years. In contrast, California has records for only 200 years. Here, geologists are studying ancient rock formations for clues to the state's earthquake history.

Space satellites and radio telescopes give information about movements of the earth's crust. Laser beams can measure changes of less than 1 inch (2.5 cm) over a distance of 10 miles (16 m). The Japanese have placed a network of instruments on the seafloor. They are also continuing to study animal behavior.

Currently, some California scientists are working on a terrascope. The terrascope will be a network of very sensitive instruments. It will be able to measure the slowest ground movements anywhere in the world. Today's seismometers don't record these silent earthquakes.

In the 1500s an astrologer predicted that during the twentieth century a "new city" would be demolished by an earthquake. In 1988, a few Californians believed the new city was Los Angeles. They were certain the earthquake would occur in May of that year, but there was no violent earthquake.

We cannot depend on myths to predict earth movement. We must rely on scientists. Only they may someday be able to give us the information we need to protect ourselves.

Glossary

aftershock—The seismic waves that occur after the main earthquake as the rock adjusts to its new position.

Carlsberg Ridge—A section of the midocean ridge.

convection currents—Currents of heat that rise, separate, cool, and descend.

convergent boundary—The line along which two plates meet.

continental crust—The crust from which our continents are formed.

core—The center of the earth.

crust—The thin outer covering of the earth.

divergent boundary—The line along which two plates are separating.

East Pacific Rise—A section of the midocean ridge.

Eurasian earthquake zone—An earthquake-prone region stretching from India to the Mediterranean Sea.

epicenter—The surface location directly above the earthquake's focus.

fault—A fracture in the earth's crust along which sections of rock are being displaced.

focus—The place where a section of rock slips and an earthquake is created.

intensity—A measure of the amount of damage caused by an earthquake.

liquefaction—The process by which loose, moist soil becomes unstable during an earthquake.

magma—Molten rock material within the earth.

magnitude—The strength or size of an earthquake.

mantle—The interior layer of the earth that is located between the crust and the core.

Mercalli scale—A means of measuring the intensity of an earthquake.

Mid-Atlantic Ridge—A section of the midocean ridge.

midocean ridge—A 40,000 mile-long underwater mountain range running down the middle of the ocean.

seismic—Pertaining to earthquakes.

seismic profiling—The process of mapping underground faults by setting off small manmade earthquakes.

seismology—The science or study of earthquakes.

submarine trenches—The underwater trenches that border the Atlantic, Pacific, and Indian oceans.

tectonic plate—One of the sections of the earth's crust.

transform boundary—The line along which two sections of crust are moving past each other in opposite directions.

tsunami—A mass of ocean water that has been put into motion.

Tsunami Warning System—A network of instruments designed to give warning of an approaching tsunami.

Further Reading

Ames, Gerald and Rose Wyler. *Restless Earth*. New York: Abelard Schuman, 1954.

Aylesworth, Thomas G. *Moving Continents: Our Changing Earth*. Hillside, N.J.: Enslow Publishers Inc., 1990.

Bain, Iain. *Mountains and Earth Movements*. New York: Bookwright Press, 1984.

Barnes-Svarney, Patricia L. *Clocks in the Rocks: Learning About Earth's Past*. Hillside, N.J.: Enslow Publishers Inc., 1990.

Earthquake. Alexandria, Va.: Time-Life Books, 1982.

Gilfond, Henry. *Disastrous Earthquakes*. New York: Franklin Watts, 1981.

Golden, Frederic. *The Trembling Earth*. New York: Scribner's, 1983.

Irving, Robert. *Volcanoes and Earthquakes*. New York: Knopf, 1962.

Lauber, Patricia. *Earthquakes*. New York: Random House, 1972.

Mercer, Charles. *Monsters in the Earth*. New York: G.P. Putnam, 1978.

Miklowitz, Gloria. *Earthquake!* New York: Julian Messner, 1977.

Oakeshott, Gordon. *Volcanoes and Earthquakes*. New York: McGraw-Hill, 1976.

Ritchie, David. *Superquake*. New York: Crown Publishers Inc., 1988.

Rutland, Jonathan. *Exploring the Violent Earth*. New York: Warwick Press, 1980.

Soren, David. "The Day the World Ended at Kourion." *National Geographic*, July, 1988, pp. 30-53.

Index